The
COOK-ZEN
Way to Eat

The
COOK-ZEN
Way to Eat

Microwaving
Healthy and
Delicious Meals
in Minutes

Machiko
Chiba

LAKE
ISLE
PRESS NEW YORK

Recipes copyright © 2010 by Machiko Chiba

MC MACHIKO ® AND COOK-ZEN ® are registered trademarks of
Machiko Cooking USA, Inc.

Food photography, copyright © 2009 Tina Rupp

Published by:
Lake Isle Press, Inc.
2095 Broadway, Suite 301
New York, NY 10023
(212) 273-0796
E-mail: lakeisle@earthlink.net

Distributed to the trade by:
National Book Network, Inc.
4501 Forbes Boulevard, Suite 200
Lanham, MD 20706
1(800) 462-6420
www.nbnbooks.com

Library of Congress Control Number: 2010926607

ISBN-13: 978-1-891105-44-9
ISBN-10: 1-891105-44-2

Photographs on page 6 reprinted with the kind permission of
Nikkei BP Kikaku Publications, Tokyo

Book and cover design: Liz Trovato

Editors: Stephanie White
        Jennifer Sit
Translator: Akiko Chiba

This book is available at special sales discounts for bulk purchases as premiums or
special editions, including customized covers. For more information, contact the
publisher at (212) 273-0796 or by e-mail, lakeisle@earthlink.net

First edition
Printed in the United States of America

10 9 8 7 6 5 4 3 2 1

Acknowledgments

The Cook-Zen microwave cook pot has truly been a labor of love, over 10 years in the making. A number of people have been instrumental in the success of the Cook-Zen and the writing of this book. First, I'd like to thank Hiroko Kiiffner, publisher of Lake Isle Press and the mastermind behind what has become an exciting and rewarding collaboration. It is because of her continuing encouragement and never-ending support that we've made it this far. Many thanks to Nozomi Terao for introducing me to Ms. Kiiffner. I would also like to mention Ms. Kiiffner's husband, Calvin. His support is constant, and his kind words are always uplifting.

My daughter, Akiko, a concert pianist in New York City, translated the recipes in this book. Her dedication to the Cook-Zen is endless—even when preparing for her own performances, she always found time to go over a recipe or help out with a cooking demo. This dedication has touched and inspired me. It's been such a blessing to publish another book together.

Once again, I was able to work with the talented photographer Tina Rupp. Her warmth and charm put us all at ease, and is reflected in her beautiful photography. Thanks, also, to Teresa Horgan, Ms. Rupp's assistant, for working tirelessly during the shoot with such efficiency and thoughtfulness. Thanks to Deborah Williams, our prop stylist, for bringing her elegant ideas to life, even when it meant carting in a heavy marble slab.

Toni Brogan, our food stylist, has truly become a Cook-Zen master. Her enthusiasm for the pot and her creativity in the kitchen make her a joy to work with. The photo shoot flew by thanks to Ms. Brogan's hard work.

Thank you to Liz Trovato, our designer, for once again bringing her unique artistry to the pages of this book. Her perspective has added so much.

Thank you to my wonderful editors at Lake Isle Press, Stephanie White and Jennifer Sit. Their months of careful editing and hard work have made this book possible.

I would also like to express gratitude to my loving and supportive family: To my dear husband, Toshio, my deepest thanks for his continuous encouragement, understanding, and unbelievable patience through the years. To my son, Keisuke, for being who you are today. And to our cats, Tora and Kuro, for their unconditional love and soothing meows.

And finally, I thank you, my readers, for giving microwave cooking another chance. I sincerely hope this book will help you make every meal a rewarding experience.

Contents

Introduction

When cookbooks first appeared on the subject of micro-wave cooking, there was great excitement. Meals prepared in minutes seemed to be the answer for busy households everywhere. The results, however, were often disappointing. Cooking in the microwave required constant stirring, and even then, ingredients cooked unevenly and came out dry and tough. Most microwaveable dishes and utensils, designed for reheating and defrosting, were not sturdy enough to cook an entire meal. There was also the inconvenience of having to take the cookware in and out of the microwave frequently just to stir. Most people gave up on the idea of microwave cooking, but I was convinced there was potential, given the right tools. As a professional chef, I set out to develop the perfect microwave pot. After ten years of experimenting and studying how microwave ovens work, I patented the Cook-Zen.

This "magic pot" cooks vegetables, rice, meat, and seafood perfectly; many of the recipes take just minutes to prepare. Made of thick, high-quality polypropylene, the Cook-Zen heats food evenly and quickly. It also seals in the moisture of your ingredients, so that they cook in their natural juices without a lot of water or oil. This means bolder flavors and more vibrant colors for everything from green beans to salmon. Besides being quick and delicious, Cook-Zen meals are healthier for you, too. Vitamins and minerals that would normally dissolve in water are retained in your foods, and the extremely short cooking times also ensure that these nutrients are better preserved.

In my first cookbook, *The Cook-Zen Cookbook*, I took on the challenge of making traditionally time-consuming and intricate Japanese dishes quickly in the microwave. In this

book, I've focused on many of the foods familiar to Western cuisine; classic comfort foods and popular take-out dishes. Chili con Carne, Caramelized Onion Soup with Mozzarella, even Asian-Style Spareribs can be made in a fraction of their traditional cooking times. These are meals you can make any night of the week. In addition to reducing prep time, I've also been able to cut out much of the oil many of these dishes usually require. The recipes are simple, quick, and delicious.

I truly believe that eating well makes people happy. May this cookbook bring you good food and happiness.

Machiko Chiba

千葉真知子

5 Good Reasons to Use the Cook-Zen

1. It's healthy.

The Cook-Zen cooks ingredients with little or no water, which means valuable vitamins and nutrients that would normally drain off are retained. And because microwave-cooking times are extremely short, more of these nutrients are preserved. Cook-Zen recipes require very little oil, for a naturally low-fat meal.

2. It's easy.

Cook-Zen recipes feature minimal ingredients that are easy to prepare. Once the pot is in the microwave, there's no need to watch over it or stir it constantly.

3. It's fast.

The Cook-Zen works like a pressure cooker, heating foods evenly and quickly. Most of the recipes take under 10 minutes to prepare.

4. It's delicious.

The Cook-Zen brings out the natural flavors of your ingredients. Meat dishes are tender and juicy, and vegetables retain their vibrant color and crispness.

5. It's safe.

Microwave cooking is perfect for teenagers and the elderly. You'll never have to worry about the risk of fire from leaving a pot or an open flame unattended.

Cook-Zen Parts

1.

2.

3.

4.

5.

1. Top Lid

The top lid has two locks that secure all of the Cook-Zen parts together. Always close these locks before cooking.

2. Middle Lid

The middle lid has patented adjustable steam holes that control whether steam is released or contained during cooking. Trapping steam in the Cook-Zen is what makes ingredients cook faster. When cooking rice recipes, we suggest setting the steam holes to "open." For other dishes, the steam holes should be set to "close."

3. Sieve

Use this sieve to rinse or drain ingredients. The sieve should not be left in the Cook-Zen when microwaving.

4. Pot

The Cook-Zen pot is made of thick polypropylene, a material that heats food evenly as it cooks. The pot can also function as a mixing bowl when you are preparing your ingredients.

5. Measuring Cup

The Cook-Zen measuring cup measures 7 fluid ounces. The recipes in this book call for both Cook-Zen cup and regular American cup measurements. Be sure to use the Cook-Zen cup where noted.

How to Use the Cook-Zen

Calibrating Your Microwave

There are many different types of microwaves on the market, with power wattages ranging from 800 to 1300 watts. All of the recipes in this book were tested on an 1100-watt microwave, with the power level set to 8, which is medium-high, or 80% of the microwave's total power. If your microwave has a lower wattage, you may need to adjust the power level when using these recipes. Follow the potato test below to determine the best settings for your microwave.

As with all methods of cooking, you will have to experiment with the Cook-Zen and your microwave to get an idea of how quickly things cook. In my own experience, even microwaves of the same model and brand name yield slightly different results. Also keep in mind that continuous use of a microwave without a break can lead to a build up of heat in the machine. This is true for conventional and toaster ovens as well. Just be mindful about shortening cooking times to account for the difference.

Potato Test

Lightly rinse a ⅓-pound potato and, leaving the peel intact, place it in the Cook-Zen. Cover the Cook-Zen and set the steam holes to "close." Place the Cook-Zen in the microwave and set the power level to 8. Heat for 4 to 5 minutes.

To test the potato, pierce it with a fork. It should go in and out of the potato smoothly. The skin should only be slightly wrinkly. If the potato is perfectly cooked, then you should follow all of the recipes as written, using power level 8.

If the potato seems undercooked, then increase the power when using these recipes to level 10, which is high, or

100% of the microwave's power. Follow the recommended cooking times.

Ingredient Notes

Bouillon Cubes

A number of recipes call for grated bouillon cubes. Bouillon cubes, or dehydrated soup stock, are great way to add flavor to recipe without adding extra liquid. Knorr is a well-known brand available in most grocery stores. Paste stocks, such as Better Than Bouillon, can also be substituted. Whichever type of bouillon you decide to use, make sure you follow the quantity called for in the recipe—that does not change no matter which variety you use.

In addition to its different forms, bouillon is also available in different flavors. The most common are chicken, beef, or vegetable. Unless otherwise indicated, you can use whichever flavor you prefer. Feel free to experiment with your own spice mixes if you prefer to use fresh herbs.

Japanese Hot Sauces and Chili Pastes

Available at Asian supermarkets, tobanjan and kochujang add unique flavors to a variety of dishes. Tobanjan is made from fermented soybeans (miso), while kochujang is essentially a red chili paste. Tabasco sauce or chili powder are both adequate substitutions for kochujang.

Sauces

Lemon-Apple Chutney

4 servings
Cook Time: 12 minutes

3 apples, peeled
$1/3$ cup white wine
Juice of 2 lemons
2 tablespoons sugar

1. Remove the cores and seeds from the apples and chop them finely.

2. Place the apples, white wine, lemon juice, and sugar in the Cook-Zen; stir well. Cover and heat on medium-high for 12 minutes with the steam holes set to "close." Serve with pork or lamb dishes.

Creamy Tomato Artichoke Sauce

2 to 4 servings
Cook Time: 9 minutes

2 cloves garlic, minced

2 tablespoons olive oil

2 artichoke hearts (canned or jarred)

2 plum tomatoes

2 to 3 anchovy fillets

$1/2$ cup heavy cream

$2/3$ tablespoon sugar

2 tablespoons minced onion

1. Place the garlic and olive oil in the Cook-Zen. Heat on medium-high, uncovered, for 40 seconds.

2. Chop the artichokes and tomatoes into small, bite-size pieces.

3. Add the remaining ingredients to the Cook-Zen, and mix well. Cover and heat on medium-high for 7 to 8 minutes with the steam holes set to "close." Serve over pasta.

Spicy Miso Sauce

4 servings
Cook Time: 4 minutes

Tobanjan, a hot sauce made from fermented soybeans (miso), gives this Asian sauce its unique flavor. Add to meat or vegetable dishes for extra heat.

1 tablespoon olive oil

1 tablespoon minced scallion

1 tablespoon minced garlic

1 tablespoon grated ginger

$1/4$ cup ketchup

$1/3$ cup chicken stock

$1/4$ cup sake

2 teaspoons sugar

1 teaspoon tobanjan (miso bean sauce)

1 tablespoon cornstarch

1. Place the olive oil, scallion, garlic, and ginger in the Cook-Zen. Heat on medium-high, uncovered, for 1 minute.

2. In the same Cook-Zen, add the remaining ingredients, and mix well. Cover and heat on medium-high for 3 minutes with the steam holes set to "close." Stir well before serving.

Garlic
Soy Sauce

2 to 4 servings
Cook Time: 3 minutes

The combination of garlic and soy is perfect for roast beef. It's also delicious with seafood.

2 cloves garlic, thinly sliced
$^1/_2$ tablespoon olive oil
$^1/_3$ to $^1/_2$ cup soy sauce

1. Place the garlic and olive oil in the Cook-Zen. Heat on medium-high, uncovered, for 40 seconds.

2. In the same Cook-Zen, add the soy sauce, cover, and heat on medium-high for 2 minutes with the steam holes set to "close." Stir before serving.

Bolognese Sauce

4 servings
Cook Time: 13 minutes

2 tablespoons olive oil

1 tablespoon minced garlic

3/4 pound ground beef

4 plum tomatoes, chopped

1 Cook-Zen cup tomato puree

5 tablespoons ketchup

1 tablespoon sugar

10 fresh basil leaves

1 medium onion, chopped

1 1/2 teaspoons grated bouillon cube, any flavor

Pinch of salt and black pepper

1. Place olive oil and garlic in the Cook-Zen and heat on high, uncovered, for 40 seconds.

2. In the same Cook-Zen, add the remaining ingredients. Mix well, cover, and heat on medium-high for 12 minutes with the steam holes set to "close." Serve over pasta.

Parsley Butter Sauce

2 servings
Cook Time: 2 minutes

Don't let the simplicity
of this sauce deceive
you—it's delicious,
especially with baked
salmon or with other
seafood.

4 tablespoons butter
1 cup minced parsley

Place the butter and parsley in the Cook-Zen. Cover and heat on medium-high for 2 to $2^1/2$ minutes with the steam holes set to "close." Stir well.

Tomato-Basil Anchovy Sauce

2 servings
Cook Time: 6 minutes

2 tablespoons olive oil

2 cloves garlic, minced

5 anchovy fillets

1 (14-ounce) can plum tomatoes with juice

6 tablespoons ketchup

5 fresh basil leaves

1^1/$_2$ tablespoons sugar

Pinch of salt and black pepper

1. Place the olive oil and garlic in the Cook-Zen. Heat on medium-high, uncovered, for 40 seconds.

2. Add the remaining ingredients to the Cook-Zen. Stir well, cover, and heat on medium-high for 5 minutes with the steam holes set to "close." Serve over pasta or with fish.

Tangy
Steak Sauce

4 to 6 servings
Cook Time: 6 minutes

Serve this sauce, a
favorite of my family,
over steak (see recipe,
page 111).

1 large onion, roughly chopped
2 cloves garlic
$^1/3$ cup soy sauce
$^1/4$ cup rice wine vinegar

1. Place the onion and garlic in a food processor and process until smooth.

2. Place the contents of the food processor, the soy sauce, and vinegar in the Cook-Zen. Mix well, cover, and heat on medium-high for 6 minutes with the steam holes set to "close." Let the sauce cool before serving.

Béchamel Sauce

2 servings
Cook Time: 3 minutes

Traditional béchamel sauce requires constant attention to keep the milk from burning. This version makes a smooth, creamy sauce without the hassle. Serve it with fish, shellfish, chicken, or pork.

1 teaspoon butter

2 tablespoons flour

^{1}/2 Cook-Zen cup milk

^{1}/2 Cook-Zen cup heavy cream

1 teaspoon grated bouillon cube, any flavor

^{1}/3 teaspoon sugar

1. Place all ingredients in the Cook-Zen and whisk well. Cover and heat on medium-high for 1^1/2 minutes with the steam holes set to "close."

2. Whisk thoroughly until smooth, cover, and heat again on medium-high for 1 to 1^1/2 minutes with the steam holes set to "close." After heating, whisk the sauce until cool.

Tomato Clam Sauce

2 servings
Cook Time: 11 minutes

1 to 1¹/4 pounds manila clams or cockles, scrubbed and rinsed
Salt
2 tablespoons olive oil
2 cloves garlic, minced
¹/4 cup white wine
2 tablespoons ketchup
1 cup tomato puree
¹/2 tablespoon sugar
1 teaspoon grated bouillon cube, any flavor
10 fresh basil leaves
Pinch of black pepper

1. Soak the clams in salted water for 30 minutes. Rinse well.

2. Place the olive oil and garlic in the Cook-Zen. Heat on medium-high, uncovered, for 40 seconds.

3. Add the remaining ingredients to the Cook-Zen. Mix well, cover, and heat on medium-high for 10 minutes with the steam holes set to "close." Serve over pasta.

Appetizers

Hummus with Mushrooms, Peppers, and Almonds

Turkish Eggplant Spread

Sundried Tomato Tapenade

Garlic-Butter Stuffed Mushrooms

Spinach Artichoke Dip

Bacon-Wrapped Avocado Scallops

Sliced Steak and Arugula Salad

Hummus with Mushrooms, Peppers, and Almonds

4 to 6 servings
Cook Time: 24 minutes

1 Cook-Zen cup dried chickpeas

7 Cook-Zen cups water

8 mushrooms

1 large red pepper

2 cloves garlic, finely chopped

$1/3$ Cook-Zen cup sliced almonds

1 teaspoon salt

$2/3$ teaspoon sugar

$1/2$ teaspoon paprika

1. Soak the chickpeas in 4 Cook-Zen cups of water until they soften, about 6 hours. After soaking, drain the water.

2. Place the chickpeas and 3 Cook-Zen cups of water in the Cook-Zen. Cover and heat on medium-high for 20 minutes with the steam holes set to "close." After heating, drain, and set the chickpeas aside.

3. Cut the mushrooms and red pepper in $1/2$-inch cubes and place them inside the Cook-Zen. Add the garlic and almonds. Cover and heat on medium-high for 4 minutes with the steam holes set to "close."

4. Transfer the contents of the Cook-Zen to a food processor, add the chickpeas and the remaining ingredients, and blend until smooth. Serve with bread, chips, or fresh vegetables.

Turkish Eggplant Spread

6 to 8 servings
Cook Time: 4 minutes

3 small Japanese eggplants, or 1 small American eggplant
   (about 8 ounces)
1 plum tomato
2 tablespoons olive oil
1/4 medium onion, finely chopped
Juice of *1/2* lemon
1 tablespoon ketchup
Pinch of salt and black pepper
Pinch of sugar

1. Place the unpeeled eggplants in the Cook-Zen. Cover and heat on medium-high for 4 minutes with the steam holes set to "close."

2. Peel the skin off the eggplants. Cut the tomato in half and remove the seeds.

3. Place all the ingredients in a food processor and pulse until thoroughly combined. Serve with bread, chips, or fresh vegetables.

Sundried Tomato Tapenade

6 to 8 servings
Cook Time: 2 minutes

3 tablespoons olive oil
2 cloves garlic, finely chopped
8 sundried tomatoes
3 capers
1 teaspoon whole grain mustard
1 anchovy fillet
$1/2$ cup finely chopped Italian parsley
8 black olives
Parmesan cheese, for garnish

1. Place all the ingredients except the Parmesan in the Cook-Zen. Cover and heat on medium-high for 2 minutes with the steam holes set to "close."

2. Place the contents of the Cook-Zen in a food processor and blend until mostly smooth. Serve on bread or crackers, and sprinkle with Parmesan cheese to garnish.

Garlic-Butter Stuffed Mushrooms

2 servings
Cook Time: 4 minutes

2 tablespoons butter
1 clove garlic, minced
1 small onion, minced
3 tablespoons grated Parmesan cheese, plus more for garnish
8 white or cremini mushrooms

1. Place the butter, garlic, onion, and 3 tablespoons Parmesan in the Cook-Zen. Cover and heat on medium-high for $1^1/2$ to 2 minutes with the steam holes set to "close."

2. Remove and discard the stems from the mushrooms. Stuff the mushroom caps with the garlic-onion mixture and sprinkle with Parmesan cheese to garnish.

3. Place the stuffed mushrooms, stuffed side up, in the Cook-Zen. Cover and heat on medium-high for $1^1/2$ to 2 minutes with the steam holes set to "close." Sprinkle with more Parmesan cheese, if desired, before serving.

Spinach Artichoke Dip

4 to 6 servings
Cook Time: 4¹/2 minutes

5 ounces baby spinach, rinsed
1 (8-ounce) bar cream cheese
¹/2 cup sour cream
4 artichoke hearts (canned or jarred), finely chopped
1 tablespoon minced garlic
Pinch of sugar
Pinch of salt and black pepper

1. Place the spinach in the Cook-Zen, cover, and heat on medium-high for 2 minutes with the steam holes set to "close." Run the cooked spinach under cool water and squeeze dry. Set aside.

2. Place the cream cheese inside the Cook-Zen. Cover and heat on medium-high for 30 seconds with the steam holes set to "close."

3. Add the spinach, sour cream, artichokes, garlic, sugar, salt, and pepper to the Cook-Zen with the cream cheese and mix well. Cover and heat on medium-high for 2 minutes with the steam holes set to "close." Let cool. Serve with crackers, bread, or fresh vegetables.

Bacon-Wrapped Avocado Scallops

2 servings

Cook Time: 2 minutes

4 large sea scallops

$^1/_2$ avocado

4 slices bacon

Cocktail picks, for serving

1. Cut the scallops horizontally, about $^3/_4$ of the way through. Remove the flesh from the avocado, and slice it into thin pieces that will fit inside the scallops. Place the avocado slices inside the scallops, and wrap each scallop with a slice of bacon. Hold the bacon in place with a cocktail pick.

2. Place the scallops in the Cook-Zen. Cover and heat on medium-high for 2 minutes with the steam holes set to "close."

Sliced Steak and Arugula Salad

4 servings
Cook Time: 4 minutes

$^1/2$ pound beef round steak
$^2/3$ Cook-Zen cup water
1 clove garlic, thinly sliced
Juice of 1 lemon
Pinch of salt
1 plum tomato, finely chopped
2 cups baby arugula, rinsed and dried
Parmesan cheese, thinly sliced, for garnish

Dressing

3 tablespoons extra virgin olive oil
2 to 3 tablespoons balsamic vinegar
Pinch of sugar
Pinch of salt and black pepper

1. Place the beef, water, garlic, lemon juice, and salt in the Cook-Zen. Cover and heat on medium-high for 4 minutes with the steam holes set to "close."

2. Remove the beef and garlic. Thinly slice the beef and arrange it with the tomatoes, arugula, garlic, and Parmesan cheese on top.

3. Make the dressing: In a small bowl, combine all ingredients and mix well. Pour the dressing over the beef and salad before serving.

Soups and Stews

Creamy Kabocha Pumpkin Soup

Minestrone

Caramelized Onion Soup with Mozzarella

Asian Vegetable and Bacon Soup

Sweet Cauliflower Soup

Clam Chowder

Garlic Fennel Soup

Spicy Chilled Tomato Soup

Smoky Napa Cabbage Bacon Soup

Adriatic Chicken-Meatball Stew

Beef and Ale Stew

Creamy Tomato Soup with Potatoes

Cherry Tomato and Mushroom Stew

Pork and Vegetable Stew

Mushroom Tarragon Soup

Tomato Basil Soup

Chili con Carne

Red Wine Stew with Chicken, Olives, and Cranberries

Corn Chowder

Creamy Kabocha Pumpkin Soup

2 servings
Cook Time: 10^1/$_2$ minutes

^{1}/$_2$ pound kabocha pumpkin
1 tablespoon butter
1 medium onion, finely chopped
^{1}/$_2$ Cook-Zen cup milk
1^1/$_2$ Cook-Zen cups heavy cream
2 teaspoons grated bouillon cube, any flavor
Pinch of salt and black pepper

1. Seed the pumpkin and cut into rough cubes. Place the pumpkin in the Cook-Zen, cover, and heat on medium-high for 5 to 6 minutes with the steam holes set to "close." Quickly remove the skin from the pumpkin and transfer the flesh to a blender. Blend until smooth.

2. Place the butter and onion in the Cook-Zen. Cover and heat on medium-high for 1^1/$_2$ minutes with the steam holes set to "close."

3. Add the butter and onions to the blender with the pumpkin. Blend until a thick paste forms. Return the paste to the Cook-Zen. Mix in the heavy cream, grated bouillon, salt, and pepper. Cover and heat on medium-high for 3 minutes with the steam holes set to "close." Stir well before serving.

Minestrone

2 servings
Cook Time: 14 minutes

1 medium potato
1 celery stalk
1 medium onion
$^1/_2$ small zucchini
$^1/_3$ medium carrot
4 mushrooms
4 string beans
$^1/_2$ plum tomato
$^1/_3$ red pepper
$^1/_3$ orange pepper
3 slices bacon
3 Cook-Zen cups water
$^1/_2$ Cook-Zen cup tomato puree
5 to 6 fresh basil leaves
1 tablespoon sugar
1$^1/_2$ teaspoons grated bouillon cube, any flavor
3 tablespoons ketchup
Pinch of salt and black pepper

1. Cut the potato, celery, onion, zucchini, carrot, mushrooms, string beans, tomato, red pepper, orange pepper, and bacon into $^1/_4$- to $^1/_2$-inch pieces. Place the vegetables and bacon in the Cook-Zen with 1 Cook-Zen cup of water. Cover and heat on medium-high for 8 minutes with the steam holes set to "close."

2. Add the remaining ingredients to the Cook-Zen. Mix well, cover, and heat on medium-high for 6 minutes with the steam holes set to "close."

Caramelized Onion Soup with Mozzarella

2 servings
Cook Time: 20 minutes

This onion soup tastes like it took hours to make. By using the Cook-Zen to start the caramelization process, you save time without losing any of the flavor.

3 large onions
2 tablespoons butter
1 clove garlic, minced
Pinch of sugar
2 Cook-Zen cups water
1 1/2 teaspoons grated bouillon cube, any flavor
1/4 cup red wine
Pinch of salt and black pepper
1/2 cup shredded mozzarella cheese

1. Peel the onions, cut in half, and julienne thinly.

2. Place the butter and garlic in the Cook-Zen. Heat on medium-high, uncovered, for 1 minute. In the same Cook-Zen, add the onion, cover, and heat on medium-high for 8 minutes with the steam holes set to "close."

3. Transfer the onion and garlic to a small frying pan over high heat. Sprinkle with sugar and sauté for 5 minutes or until onions and garlic become caramelized.

4. Return the onions and garlic to the Cook-Zen. Add the water, grated bouillon, red wine, salt, and pepper. Cover and heat on medium-high for 5 minutes with the steam holes set to "close."

5. Pour the onion soup into 2 small, microwave-safe bowls. Sprinkle the mozzarella cheese on top of each bowl and heat on medium-high for 1 minute or until the cheese is melted.

Asian Vegetable and Bacon Soup

2 servings
Cook Time: 13 minutes

You can taste all the natural goodness of the vegetables in this gentle soup.

1 daikon or white radish (about $^1/4$-pound)
$^1/2$ medium carrot
1 shiitake mushroom
10 snow peas
3 slices bacon
3 Cook-Zen cups water
3 teaspoons grated bouillon cubes, any flavor
Pinch of salt and black pepper

1. Thinly julienne the daikon, carrot, mushroom, snow peas, and bacon. Place the daikon, carrot, mushroom, and bacon inside the Cook-Zen and add 1 Cook-Zen cup of water. Cover and heat on medium-high for 8 minutes with the steam holes set to "close."

2. In the same Cook-Zen, add 2 Cook-Zen cups of water, the grated bouillon, and snow peas. Cover and heat on medium-high for 5 minutes with the steam holes set to "close." Mix well, adding a pinch of salt and black pepper to taste.

Sweet Cauliflower Soup

2 servings
Cook Time: 21 minutes

1 small head cauliflower (about $^1/4$ pound)
1 tablespoon butter
1 medium onion, finely chopped
$^1/2$ Cook-Zen cup water
1 Cook-Zen cup heavy cream
$^2/3$ Cook-Zen cup milk
2 teaspoons grated bouillon cube, any flavor
Pinch of sugar

1. Chop the cauliflower into florets. Place the florets in the Cook-Zen, cover, and heat on medium-high for 10 minutes with the steam holes set to "close." Remove the cauliflower from the Cook-Zen and set aside to cool.

2. Place the butter and onion inside the Cook-Zen. Cover and heat on medium-high for 3 minutes with the steam holes set to "close."

3. Place the cauliflower and onion in a food processor and blend until smooth. Place the cauliflower mixture and remaining ingredients in the Cook-Zen. Mix well, cover, and heat on medium-high for 4 to 5 minutes with the steam holes set to "close."

Clam Chowder

2 servings
Cook Time: 9 minutes

$^1/_2$ pound small clams or cockles, scrubbed and rinsed.
Salt
1 tablespoon butter
1 medium onion, finely chopped
1 Cook-Zen cup heavy cream
1 tablespoon flour
$1^1/_2$ Cook-Zen cups milk
$^1/_3$ cup mixed vegetables, fresh or frozen
Pinch of black pepper
Pinch of sugar
$1^1/_2$ teaspoons grated bouillon cube, any flavor

1. Soak the clams in salted water for 30 minutes. Rinse well.

2. Place the butter and onion in the Cook-Zen. Cover and heat on medium-high for 3 minutes with the steam holes set to "close."

3. Pour the heavy cream into a small mixing bowl. Sieve the flour into the cream to avoid any lumps. Mix well.

4. In the Cook-Zen, add the cream mixture, clams, and remaining ingredients to the onions. Stir well. Cover and heat on medium-high for 6 minutes with the steam holes set to "close." Add a pinch of salt, to taste.

Garlic Fennel Soup

4 servings
Cook Time: 10 minutes

2 cloves garlic, minced

2 tablespoons olive oil

1 medium onion, minced

1 small fennel bulb, without the fronds, finely chopped

3 Cook-Zen cups water

1 Cook-Zen cup heavy cream

$2^1/2$ to 3 teaspoons grated bouillon cube, any flavor

Pinch of sugar

Pinch of celery seeds

Pinch of salt and black pepper

1. Place the garlic and olive oil in the Cook-Zen. Heat on medium-high, uncovered, for 40 seconds.

2. Add the onion and fennel to the Cook-Zen. Cover and heat on medium-high for 3 minutes with the steam holes set to "close." Add the remaining ingredients and mix well. Cover and heat on medium-high for 6 minutes with the steam holes set to "close." Run the soup through a sieve before serving to remove any large pieces.

Spicy Chilled Tomato Soup

2 servings
Cook Time: 5 minutes
plus 1 hour for cooling

1 green chile pepper
2 large tomatoes, diced
$1/2$ teaspoon ground cumin seeds
Pinch of salt and black pepper
Pinch of sugar
1 cup coconut milk
$1/2$ cup heavy cream

1. Cut the chile pepper along the side, removing the seeds with caution (see Note). Place the chile pepper, tomatoes, cumin, salt, pepper, and sugar in the Cook-Zen. Cover and heat on medium-high for 5 minutes with the steam holes set to "close."

2. Transfer the contents of the Cook-Zen to a food processor. Add the coconut milk and heavy cream and pulse until smooth. Strain the soup through a sieve and refrigerate until cool, about 1 hour. Stir well before serving.

Note: Be careful when working with chiles; the natural oils can burn. Don't touch your eyes, and wash your hands immediately after handling.

Smoky Napa Cabbage Bacon Soup

2 servings
Cook Time: 6 minutes

6 to 8 Napa cabbage leaves (about $1/2$ pound)
3 slices bacon
2 Cook-Zen cups water
1 to $1^1/2$ teaspoons grated bouillon cube, any flavor
Pinch of black pepper

1. Juilenne the cabbage and bacon into $1/4$-inch strips.

2. Place the cabbage, bacon, water, and grated bouillon in the Cook-Zen. Cover and heat on medium-high for 6 minutes with the steam holes set to "close." Sprinkle with black pepper before serving.

Adriatic Chicken-Meatball Stew

2 servings
Cook Time: 15 minutes

$^1/_2$ celery stalk

1 small zucchini

3 plum tomatoes

$^1/_2$ small head broccoli (about $^1/_3$ pound)

$^1/_3$ pound ground chicken

1 tablespoon olive oil

2 cloves garlic, sliced

1 teaspoon grated bouillon cube, any flavor

2 tablespoons red wine vinegar

5 tablespoons ketchup

1 red chile pepper, finely chopped

Pinch of salt and black pepper

1 teaspoon sugar

1. Cut the celery and zucchini in $^1/_2$-inch slices. Halve each tomato and cut into wedges. Chop the broccoli into florets.

2. Place the broccoli in the Cook-Zen. Cover and heat on medium-high for 2 minutes with the steam holes set to "close." Transfer the broccoli to a small bowl and set aside.

3. Place the ground chicken inside a bowl and knead well. Form into 1-inch balls.

4. Place the olive oil and garlic in the Cook-Zen and heat, uncovered, on medium-high for 1 minute. Add the zucchini, celery, chicken balls, tomatoes, grated bouillon, vinegar, ketchup, chile pepper, salt, pepper, and sugar. Cover and heat on medium-high for 10 to 12 minutes with the steam holes set to "close." Add the broccoli and mix gently before serving.

Beef and Ale Stew

2 servings
Cook Time: 25 minutes

This stew, popular in Germany, works well with leftover beer.

1 small potato, any kind
2 tablespoons olive oil
2 cloves garlic, sliced
2 small onions, finely chopped
$^1/_2$ pound beef round steak
1 small carrot
2 plum tomatoes
4 mushrooms, thinly sliced
2 teaspoons grated bouillon cube, any flavor
Pinch of marjoram
1 cup beer
1 teaspoon paprika
Pinch of salt and black pepper
Pinch of sugar
4 tablespoons sour cream

1. Place the potato, unpeeled, in the Cook-Zen. Cover and heat on medium-high for 4 to 5 minutes with the steam holes set to "close." After heating, peel the potato and cut into bite-size pieces. Set aside.

2. Place the olive oil, garlic, and onions in the Cook-Zen. Cover and heat on medium-high for 2$^1/_2$ minutes with the steam holes set to "close."

3. Cut the beef into 1-inch long slices, the carrots into $^1/_2$-inch slices, and the tomatoes into $^1/_2$-inch cubes.

4. Add the beef, carrots, tomatoes, mushrooms, grated bouillon, marjoram, beer, paprika, salt, pepper, and sugar to the Cook-Zen with the onions and garlic. Cover and heat on medium-high for 12 to 13 minutes with the steam holes set to "close."

5. Mix in the sour cream, cover, and heat on medium-high for 5 minutes with the steam holes set to "close." Add the potatoes and gently mix before serving.

Creamy Tomato Soup with Potatoes

2 servings
Cook Time: 20 minutes

2 medium potatoes, any kind

1 medium onion

$^1/_2$ medium carrot

$^1/_3$ celery stalk

2 plum tomatoes, diced

1 tablespoon butter

1 Cook-Zen cup heavy cream

1 teaspoon sugar

2 teaspoons grated bouillon cube, any flavor

1. Place the potatoes, unpeeled, in the Cook-Zen. Cover and heat on medium-high for 8 minutes with the steam holes set to "close." After heating, remove potatoes from the Cook-Zen, peel, and set aside.

2. Peel the onion and carrot and cut into small, rough chunks. Cut the celery into rough chunks and place the onion, carrot, celery, and butter in the Cook-Zen. Cover and heat on medium-high for 4 to 5 minutes with the steam holes set to "close." After heating, place the contents of the Cook-Zen in a food processor. Add the tomatoes and potatoes and pulse until smooth.

3. Return the vegetable mixture to the Cook-Zen and add the heavy cream, sugar, and grated bouillon. Mix well. Cover and heat on medium-high for 6 to 7 minutes with the steam holes set to "close."

Cherry Tomato and Mushroom Stew

2 servings

Cook Time: 6 minutes

$1/4$ pound white or cremini mushrooms, stems removed

3 tablespoons ketchup

3 tablespoons water

$1/2$ tablespoon sugar

1 teaspoon kochujang (red chili paste), see Note

1 teaspoon grated bouillon cube, any flavor

Pinch of salt and black pepper

$1/2$ pound cherry tomatoes

1 small onion, finely chopped

5 to 6 fresh basil leaves, finely chopped

Parmesan cheese, grated, for garnish

Place all the ingredients, except the Parmesan, in the Cook-Zen and mix well. Cover and heat on medium-high for 5 to 6 minutes with the steam holes set to "close." Garnish with Parmesan cheese before serving.

Note: Although the flavor will be different, you can substitute a pinch of chili powder or a few drops of Tabasco sauce for the kochujang.

Pork and Vegetable Stew

2 servings
Cook Time: 16 minutes

5 small potatoes, any kind
$1/2$ celery stalk
1 small zucchini
1 red pepper
$1/4$ pound pork tenderloin
1 tablespoon olive oil
1 tablespoon minced garlic
5 pearl onions, peeled
5 baby carrots, halved
10 cherry tomatoes, quartered
5 mushrooms
3 tablespoons tomato puree
3 to 4 tablespoons ketchup
$1^1/2$ teaspoons grated bouillon cube, any flavor
1 teaspoon sugar
Pinch of salt and black pepper
Pinch of fresh basil leaves
Parmesan cheese, thinly sliced, for garnish

1. Place the potatoes, unpeeled, in the Cook-Zen. Cover and heat on medium-high for 3 minutes with the steam holes set to "close." After cooling, peel the potatoes and cut into bite-size pieces. Set aside.

2. Cut the celery and zucchini into $1/2$-inch slices, the red pepper into 1-inch cubes, and the pork into bite-size pieces.

3. Place the olive oil and garlic in the Cook-Zen, and heat on medium-high, uncovered, for 1 minute.

4. Add the remaining ingredients, except for the potatoes and Parmesan to the Cook-Zen and mix well. Cover and heat on medium-high for 12 minutes with the steam holes set to "close." Add the potatoes and gently mix. Garnish with Parmesan slices before serving.

Mushroom Tarragon Soup

2 servings
Cook Time: 9 minutes

1 tablespoon olive oil

1 clove garlic, minced

$^1/_2$ medium onion, finely chopped

$^1/_2$ cup finely chopped fresh tarragon

8 to 10 mushrooms, thinly sliced

$^1/_2$ Cook-Zen cup water

1 Cook-Zen cup heavy cream

1 tablespoon butter

2 teaspoons grated bouillon cube, any flavor

Pinch of sugar

1. Place the olive oil and garlic in the Cook-Zen. Heat on medium-high, uncovered, for 40 seconds.

2. Place the onions, tarragon, and mushrooms in the Cook-Zen with the olive oil and garlic. Cover and heat on medium-high for 3 minutes with the steam holes set to "close."

3. Add the remaining ingredients and mix well. Cover and heat on medium-high for 5 minutes with the steam holes set to "close."

Tomato Basil Soup

2 servings
Cook Time: 8 minutes

The flavor of this soup intensifies when you use ripe tomatoes. This soup can also be used as a sauce for pasta dishes.

4 large tomatoes
2^1/2 tablespoons finely chopped fresh basil leaves
1^1/2 teaspoons grated bouillon cube, any flavor
^{1}/2 tablespoon sugar

1. Place the tomatoes in the Cook-Zen, cover, and heat on medium-high for 5 to 6 minutes with the steam holes set to "close."

2. Remove the tomatoes and place them inside a sieve. Place the Cook-Zen below the sieve and flatten the tomatoes to separate the juice and the peel. Discard the peel and seeds, but keep the juice in the Cook-Zen.

3. Add the basil, grated bouillon, and sugar to the Cook-Zen, and mix well with the tomato juice. Cover and heat on medium-high for 2 minutes with the steam holes set to "close."

Chili con Carne

2 servings
Cook Time: 16 minutes

4 cloves garlic, minced

1 tablespoon olive oil

$^1/_2$ pound ground beef

1 medium onion, finely chopped

1 green chile pepper or jalapeño, seeds removed, and
    chopped, see Note

$^1/_2$ Cook-Zen cup canned kidney beans

1 tablespoon hot chili powder

1 tablespoon sweet paprika

$^1/_2$ teaspoon ground cumin

$^1/_2$ teaspoon dried oregano

2 large tomatoes, finely chopped

$^1/_2$ large red pepper, finely chopped

1 teaspoon bouillon cube, any flavor

1 tablespoon sugar

Pinch of cinnamon

Pinch of salt and black pepper

Grated cheddar cheese, for garnish

1. Place the garlic and olive oil in the Cook-Zen. Heat on medium-high, uncovered, for 40 seconds.

2. Add the remaining ingredients to the Cook-Zen and mix well. Cover and heat on medium-high for 15 minutes with the stream holes set to "close." Sprinkle with cheddar cheese before serving.

Note: Be careful when working with chiles; the natural oils can burn. Don't touch your eyes, and wash your hands immediately after handling.

Red Wine Stew with Chicken, Olives, and Cranberries

2 servings
Cook Time: 16 minutes

1 tablespoon olive oil

$^1/2$ small onion, finely chopped

6 pearl onions, peeled

$^1/2$ pound boneless chicken breast, diced

8 black olives

3 tablespoons dried cranberries

$^3/4$ cup tomato puree

$^1/2$ cup red wine

4 tablespoons ketchup

1 tablespoon paprika

$1^1/2$ tablespoons sugar

1 teaspoon grated bouillon cube, any flavor

4 fresh basil leaves

1 sprig rosemary

Pinch of salt and pepper

1. Place the olive oil and all the onions in the Cook-Zen. Heat on medium-high, uncovered, for 1 minute.

2. Add the remaining ingredients to the Cook-Zen and mix well. Cover and heat on medium-high for 15 minutes with the steam holes set to "close." Serve with crusty bread.

Corn Chowder

2 servings

Cook Time: 8 minutes

¹/2 medium onion, finely chopped

2 tablespoons butter

1 Cook-Zen cup milk

³/4 Cook-Zen cup heavy cream

1¹/2 teaspoons grated bouillon cube

1 Cook-Zen cup canned cream corn

1 Cook-Zen cup canned corn kennels

A pinch of salt and black pepper

1. Place the onion and butter in the Cook-Zen, cover, and heat on medium-high for 3 minutes with the steam holes set to "close." Mix well.

2. Add the milk, heavy cream, grated bouillon, and both canned corns to the Cook-Zen, mixing well. Cover and heat on medium-high for 5 minutes with the steam holes set to "close."

Main Dishes

Beef and Tofu Sliders

Korean Beef Bulgogi

Steak Teriyaki

Creamy Dill Shrimp

Garlic Lime Chicken

Spicy Pork Tenderloin with Potatoes and Onions

Sea Bass Pot-au-Feu

Chicken Curry with Spinach and Apple

Salmon with Lemon-Soy Sauce

Seafood Bouillabaisse

Sloppy Joes

Chicken, Basil, and Anchovy Sauté

Mussels Steamed with Wine and Garlic

Chicken with Tomato-Basil Sauce

Baked or Boiled Sausages with Cabbage

Thai Green Curry Chicken

Scallop Pilaf with Vegetables

Spicy Shrimp with Peas

Paella

Yellow Curry

Asian-Style Spareribs

Stuffed Calamari

Simmered Beef

Beef Round Steak with Garlic

Salmon Teriyaki

Spicy Coconut Chicken

Beef and Tofu Sliders

Makes 4 sliders
Cook Time: 4¹/2 minutes

Mixing the beef with tofu makes these sliders healthier and every bit as delicious as traditional sliders.

¹/2 small onion, finely chopped
¹/2 tablespoon butter
¹/2 pound ground beef
¹/3 block medium-firm tofu, gently crumbled and drained (about 4 ounces)
2 tablespoons cornstarch plus 2 teaspoons
1 teaspoon sugar plus 4 tablespoons
Pinch of salt
6 tablespoons soy sauce
Drop of sesame oil
4 small hamburger buns, for serving

1. Place the onion and butter in the Cook-Zen. Cover and heat on medium-high for 1 minute with the steam holes set to "close." Transfer the onions to a small bowl to cool.

2. In a separate bowl, knead the beef until it has a smooth texture. Add the tofu, onion, 2 tablespoons cornstarch, 1 teaspoon sugar, and salt and continue kneading until combined. Divide the meat into 4 balls and flatten each into a patty.

3. In a small bowl, place the soy sauce, remaining 2 teaspoons cornstarch, 4 tablespoons sugar, and sesame oil. Mix well.

4. Place two patties in the Cook-Zen and cover with half the soy sauce mixture. Cover and heat on medium-high for 3 to 3¹/2 minutes with the steam holes set to "close." Repeat with remaining two sliders. Serve on buns with your favorite toppings.

Korean Beef Bulgogi

2 servings
Cook Time: 5 minutes

A classic Korean dish, beef bulgogi is prepared here without the use of the open flame which gives the dish it's name: fire meat.

6 tablespoons soy sauce

3 tablespoons sugar

3 tablespoons ground white sesame seeds

1 teaspoon finely chopped scallion plus $^1/_2$ scallion

1 teaspoon minced garlic

$^1/_2$ pear, grated

1 tablespoon kochujang (red chili paste)

1 teaspoon red pepper flakes

$^1/_3$ pound beef round steak, thinly sliced

$^1/_2$ medium onion

$^1/_2$ carrot

1 green pepper

2 shiitake mushrooms

5 bunches Asian chives (about $^1/_3$ pound)

1 teaspoon olive oil

Pinch of white sesame seeds

1. In a medium bowl, mix the soy sauce, sugar, sesame seeds, chopped scallion, garlic, pear, kochujang, and red pepper flakes. Add the beef to the bowl and let marinate for 15 minutes.

2. Thinly julienne the onion, carrot, pepper, and shiitake mushrooms into 1 x $^1/_4$-inch pieces. Cut the scallion and chives into 1-inch pieces.

3. Place the olive oil, beef with marinade, vegetables, and sesame seeds in the Cook-Zen; mix well. Cover and heat on medium-high for 5 minutes with the steam holes set to "close." Serve over rice.

Steak Teriyaki

2 *servings*
Cook Time: $6^1/2$ *minutes*

Teriyaki sauce has a tendency to burn when cooked. By using the Cook-Zen, there's no risk of burning. You're left with juicy meat and plenty of delicious sauce.

2 teaspoons olive oil

1 clove garlic, minced

$^1/2$ to $^3/4$ pound sirloin steak, thinly sliced

3 to 4 tablespoons soy sauce

1 tablespoon mirin

1 to $1^1/2$ tablespoons sugar

$^1/2$ teaspoon black pepper

$^1/2$ tablespoon cornstarch

2 tablespoons water

1. Place the olive oil and garlic in the Cook-Zen. Heat on medium-high, uncovered, for 40 seconds.

2. Add the beef, soy sauce, mirin, sugar, and black pepper. Cover and heat on medium-high for 4 to 5 minutes with the steam holes set to "close." Set the beef aside, leaving the sauce inside the Cook-Zen.

3. In a small bowl, mix the cornstarch and water. Add the cornstarch mixture to the sauce in the Cook-Zen. Stir well. Heat on medium-high, uncovered, for 30 seconds. Whisk the sauce thoroughly. Pour over the beef before serving.

Creamy Dill Shrimp

2 to 3 servings
Cook Time: 4 minutes

1 pound large shrimp

3 tablespoons white wine

1 tablespoon finely chopped dill

3 to 4 tablespoons heavy cream

3 to 4 tablespoons mayonnaise

1 celery stalk, minced

1. Place the shrimp in the Cook-Zen, leaving the shells and tails intact. Sprinkle the white wine over the shrimp, cover, and heat on medium-high for 4 minutes with the steam holes set to "close."

2. Peel and devein the shrimp after heating, and place them in a separate mixing bowl. Add the remaining ingredients and mix gently.

Garlic Lime Chicken

3 *servings*

Cook Time: 6 minutes

2/3 pound boneless chicken breast, cubed

1/4 cup fresh lime juice

2 tablespoons olive oil

2 tablespoons minced garlic

Pinch of salt and black pepper

6 capers

5 black olives, sliced

1. Place the chicken in the Cook-Zen and sprinkle with lime juice. Rub the olive oil, garlic, salt, and pepper into the meat. Marinate for 30 minutes.

2. Add the capers and olives, cover, and heat on medium-high for 6 minutes with the steam holes set to "close." Stir gently before serving.

Spicy Pork Tenderloin with Potatoes and Onions

2 servings
Cook Time: 15 minutes

2 medium potatoes, any kind
$^1/_4$ pound boneless pork tenderloin
2 small onions
1 tablespoon olive oil
1 tablespoon butter
1 tablespoon minced garlic
2 tablespoons soy sauce
$1^1/_2$ tablespoons sugar
1 teaspoon chili paste
Pinch of red peppercorns

1. Place the potatoes, unpeeled, inside the Cook-Zen. Cover and heat on medium-high for 8 to 9 minutes with the steam holes set to "close." After heating, peel the potatoes and cut them into bite-size pieces. Set aside.

2. Cut the pork into $^1/_2$-inch thick slices, then cut again to make $^1/_2$ x 1-inch pieces. Peel the onions and cut it into $^1/_2$-inch pieces.

3. Place the pork, onions, olive oil, butter, garlic, soy sauce, sugar, and chili paste in the Cook-Zen and mix well. Cover and heat on medium-high for 5 to 6 minutes with the steam holes set to "close."

4. Add the potatoes and gently mix. Sprinkle with red peppercorns before serving.

Sea Bass Pot-au-Feu

2 servings
Cook Time: 19 minutes

1 medium potato, any kind
2 tablespoons olive oil
2 cloves garlic, sliced
$^1/_2$ small head cabbage
1 medium onion
$^1/_2$ celery stalk
1 medium carrot
1 red pepper
3 slices bacon
1 small zucchini
1 ($^1/_2$-pound) sea bass fillet, no skin
1$^1/_2$ cups water
2 teaspoons grated bouillon cube, any flavor
Pinch of salt and black pepper

1. Place the potato, unpeeled, in the Cook-Zen, cover, and heat on medium-high for 4 minutes with the steam holes set to "close." Peel the skin, and cut the potato into bite-size pieces. Set aside.

2. Place the olive oil and garlic in the Cook-Zen, and heat on medium-high, uncovered, for 40 seconds.

3. Shred the cabbage; cut the onion, celery, carrot, and red pepper into 1-inch cubes, and place everything in the Cook-Zen. Slice the bacon into $^1/_4$-inch pieces and add to the Cook-Zen. Cover and heat on medium-high for 10 minutes with the steam holes set to "close."

4. Cut the zucchini and sea bass into 1-inch chunks, and add to the Cook-Zen. Add the water, grated bouillon, salt, and black pepper, cover, and heat on medium-high for 5 minutes with the steam holes set to "close." Add the potato and gently mix before serving.

Chicken Curry with Spinach and Apple

2 servings
Cook Time: 18 minutes

2 cloves garlic, minced

$^1/_2$ medium onion, finely chopped

2 tablespoons olive oil

$^1/_2$ apple, diced

1 plum tomato, diced

$^1/_4$ pound boneless chicken breast, diced into $^3/_4$-inch cubes

12 ounces spinach, rinsed and cut into strips

2 teaspoons grated bouillon cube, any flavor

2 tablespoons ketchup

1 tablespoon sugar

2 tablespoons sour cream

3 tablespoons heavy cream

$^1/_4$ teaspoon marjoram

$^1/_4$ teaspoon cayenne pepper

$^1/_4$ teaspoon chili powder

4 cardamom pods

$^1/_8$ teaspoon dried oregano

$^1/_4$ teaspoon dried basil leaves

$^1/_2$ teaspoon paprika

$^1/_4$ teaspoon black pepper

Pinch of salt

1. Place the garlic, onion, and olive oil in the Cook-Zen. Cover and heat on medium-high for 3 minutes with the steam holes set to "close."

2. Add the apple, tomato, chicken, and spinach to the contents of the Cook-Zen. Cover and heat on medium-high for 10 minutes with the steam holes set to "close."

3. Add the remaining ingredients to the Cook-Zen and mix well. Cover and heat on medium-high for 5 minutes with the steam holes set to "close."

Salmon with Lemon-Soy Sauce

1 serving
Cook Time: 2^1/2 to 3
minutes

1 (^{1}/2-pound) salmon fillet, with skin
Pinch of salt
Juice of 1 lemon
2 tablespoons soy sauce
2 tablespoons olive oil
^{1}/2 tablespoon sugar

1. Lightly sprinkle the salmon with salt. Place the salmon in the Cook-Zen, cover, and heat on medium-high for 2^1/2 to 3 minutes with the steam holes set to "close."

2. In a small bowl, combine the lemon juice, soy sauce, olive oil, and sugar. Mix well. Pour the lemon dressing over the salmon before serving.

Seafood Bouillabaisse

2 servings
Cook Time: 9 minutes

2 tablespoons olive oil

2 cloves garlic, minced

2 large shrimp, heads intact

2 (2-ounce) squid, cleaned and cut into $^1/_2$-inch rings

5 mussels

6 small bay scallops

1 plum tomato, chopped

10 fresh basil leaves

Pinch of saffron

2 anchovy fillets

1 teaspoon grated bouillon cube, any flavor

Pinch of salt and black pepper

Pinch of sugar

2 tablespoons ketchup

1 Cook-Zen cup water

1. Place the olive oil and garlic in the Cook-Zen. Heat on medium-high, uncovered, for 50 seconds.

2. Add the remaining ingredients and mix well. Cover and heat on medium-high for 7 to 8 minutes with the steam holes set to "close." Stir gently before serving.

Sloppy Joes

4 servings
Cook Time: 10 minutes

3/4 pound ground beef
2 cloves garlic, minced
1 tablespoon olive oil
1 medium onion, finely chopped
1/2 green pepper, seeded and finely chopped
3 plum tomatoes, finely chopped
2 1/2 tablespoons tomato paste
1 tablespoon white vinegar
1 tablespoon sugar
1 1/2 teaspoons cayenne pepper
4 to 5 whole cloves
1 tablespoon ketchup
Pinch of salt and black pepper
4 hamburger buns, for serving
4 scallions, finely chopped, for garnish

1. Place the beef and garlic in the Cook-Zen. Cover and heat on medium-high for 5 minutes with the stream holes set to "close." After heating, place the meat in the sieve to drain excess water and fat.

2. Return the beef and garlic to the Cook-Zen. Add the remaining ingredients and mix well. Cover and heat on medium-high for 5 minutes with the stream holes set to "close."

3. Remove the whole cloves from the sloppy joes and serve on hamburger buns. Garnish with scallions.

Chicken, Basil, and Anchovy Sauté

2 servings

Cook Time: 7 minutes

1 tablespoon olive oil

2 cloves garlic, sliced

$1/2$ pound chicken breast, cubed

3 to 4 anchovy fillets

2 plum tomatoes, diced

10 fresh basil leaves

Parmesan cheese, grated, for garnish

1. Place the olive oil and garlic inside the Cook-Zen. Heat on medium-high, uncovered, for 40 seconds.

2. Add the remaining ingredients, except the Parmesan, to the Cook-Zen with the garlic and mix well. Cover and heat on medium-high for 5 to 6 minutes with the steam holes set to "close." Sprinkle with Parmesan cheese before serving.

Mussels Steamed with Wine and Garlic

2 servings
Cook Time: 7 minutes

1^1/4 pounds mussels
2 tablespoons olive oil
2 cloves garlic, minced
^{1}/2 cup white wine
Pinch of salt and black pepper

1. Place the mussels in a bowl and rinse under cool running water. Drain well.

2. Place the olive oil and garlic in the Cook-Zen, and heat on medium-high, uncovered, for 40 seconds. Add the mussels, wine, salt, and pepper. Cover and heat on medium-high for 6 minutes with the steam holes set to "close."

Chicken with Tomato-Basil Sauce

2 servings
Cook Time: 11 minutes

1 tablespoon olive oil

1 clove garlic, minced

$1/2$ pound boneless chicken breast, cubed

10 fresh basil leaves

1 cup red wine

1 (14-ounce) can whole tomatoes, drained

4 tablespoons ketchup

2 tablespoons sugar

2 teaspoons grated bouillon cube, any flavor

Pinch of black pepper

1. Place the olive oil and garlic in the Cook-Zen. Heat on medium-high, uncovered, for 40 seconds.

2. Add the remaining ingredients to the Cook-Zen and mix well. Cover and heat on medium-high for 10 minutes with the steam holes set to "close."

Baked or Boiled Sausages with Cabbage

3 servings

Cook Time: 5 to 7 minutes

6 small sausages, raw

$^1/3$ cup water (for boiling sausage)

6 cabbage leaves or fresh lettuce, optional

Whole grain mustard, for serving

1. For boiled sausage: Place the sausages and water in the Cook-Zen. Cover and heat on medium-high for 2 to 3 minutes with the steam holes set to "close." Set sausages aside.

2. For baked sausage: Place sausages in the Cook-Zen, and heat on medium-high for 1 to 1$^1/2$ minutes with the steam holes set to "close." Set sausages aside.

3. Make the cabbage: Place the cabbage leaves in the Cook-Zen. Cover and heat on medium-high for 3 to 4 minutes with the steam holes set to "close."

4. Serve each sausage on a cabbage leaf topped with mustard, to taste.

Thai Green Curry Chicken

2 servings
Cook Time: 17 minutes

1 medium potato, any kind

$1/3$ pound chicken thigh, skin on

1 Japanese eggplant or $1/2$ small American eggplant

$1/2$ green pepper

$1/2$ red pepper

1 medium onion

2 tablespoons olive oil

2 Cook-Zen cups water

4 tablespoons Thai green curry paste

1 teaspoon grated bouillon cube, any flavor

4 tablespoons coconut milk

2 teaspoons sugar

$1/2$ teaspoon fish sauce

3 to 4 lime leaves

1 sprig lemon grass

1. Place the potato in the Cook-Zen, unpeeled. Cover and heat on medium-high for 5 minutes with the steam holes set to "close." Peel the skin, and cut the potato into bite-size pieces. Set aside.

2. Cut the chicken into bite-size pieces. Cut the eggplant, green and red peppers, and onion into $1/2$ x $1 1/2$-inch pieces. Place the olive oil, eggplant, green pepper, red pepper, onion, and chicken inside the Cook-Zen. Cover and heat on medium-high for 4 to 5 minutes with the steam holes set to "close."

3. Add the remaining ingredients to the Cook-Zen and mix gently. Cover and heat on medium-high for 6 to 7 minutes with the steam holes set to "close." Add the potato and toss gently before serving.

Scallop Pilaf with Vegetables

2 servings
Cook Time: 16 minutes

2 Cook-Zen cups white rice

2^1/2 Cook-Zen cups water

4 large sea scallops

^{1}/2 medium carrot

^{1}/2 green pepper

^{1}/4 yellow pepper

^{1}/4 medium onion

5 pearl onions

2 tablespoons butter

1^1/2 teaspoons grated bouillon cube, any flavor

1. Place the rice in the Cook-Zen, add fresh cold water to cover, and swish the rice around to wash. Drain and repeat several times until the water runs clear. Drain the rice well. Add 2^1/2 Cook-Zen cups water and let soak for 1 hour. Do not drain.

2. Quarter the scallops. Finely chop the carrots, green pepper, yellow pepper, and onion. Peel and cut the pearl onions into quarters.

3. Add the scallops, carrots, green and yellow peppers, onions, butter, and grated bouillon to the Cook-Zen with the rice and water, and mix well. Cover and heat on medium-high for 16 minutes with the steam holes set to "open."

Spicy Shrimp with Peas

2 servings
Cook Time: 10 minutes

10 ounces large shrimp

1^1/2 tablespoons sake

1 tablespoon olive oil

1 tablespoon minced garlic

1 tablespoon minced ginger

1 tablespoon minced scallion

^{1}/2 cup ketchup

1^1/2 to 2 tablespoons sugar

1 teaspoon chili paste

^{1}/4 cup water

^{1}/2 teaspoon grated chicken-flavored bouillon cube

^{1}/2 teaspoon cornstarch

^{1}/4 cup frozen peas

1. Shell and devein the shrimp, leaving the tails intact. Sprinkle the shrimp with sake and let them marinate for a few minutes.

2. Place the olive oil, garlic, ginger, and scallion in the Cook-Zen and heat, uncovered, for 1^1/2 minutes. Add the remaining ingredients except the peas. Cover and heat on medium-high for 5 to 6 minutes with the steam holes set to "close." Stir in the peas, and let stand for 2 to 3 minutes with the lids closed. Mix well before serving.

Paella

2 servings
Cook Time: 22 minutes

1 Cook-Zen cup white rice
1 Cook-Zen cup water
1 artichoke heart (canned or jarred)
4 stalks asparagus
10 string beans
3 tablespoons olive oil
2 cloves garlic, minced
1 medium onion, finely chopped
4 cherry tomatoes
6 medium shrimp
3 anchovy fillets
4 large sea scallops
6 mussels
3 tablespoons ketchup
1 fresh basil leaf
Pinch of oregano
Pinch of saffron
1 tablespoon butter
1 tablespoon minced celery
1 teaspoon grated bouillon cube, any flavor

1. Place the rice in a medium bowl, add fresh cold water to cover, and swish the rice around to wash. Drain and repeat several times until the water runs clear. Drain the rice well. Add 1 Cook-Zen cup of water and let soak for at least 30 minutes.

2. Cut the artichoke heart into 8 slices, and the asparagus and string beans into 1-inch pieces.

3. Place the olive oil, garlic, and onion in the Cook-Zen. Cover and heat on medium-high for 2 minutes with the steam holes set to "close."

4. Add the rice with its water and the remaining ingredients to the Cook-Zen. Cover and heat on medium-high for 20 minutes with the steam holes set to "open." Stir well before serving.

Yellow Curry

2 servings
Cook Time: 26 minutes

1 medium potato, any kind

1 tablespoon olive oil

2 cloves garlic, minced

1 large onion, finely chopped

^{1}/3 celery stalk, finely chopped

1 tablespoon freshly grated ginger

1 medium carrot, diced

1 Japanese eggplant or ^{1}/2 small American eggplant, diced

3 to 4 mushrooms, stems removed

1 small head broccoli (about 3 ounces), cut into florets

2 ounces ground pork, beef, or chicken

^{1}/2 Cook-Zen cup water

1^1/2 tablespoons curry powder

^{1}/2 teaspoon cayenne pepper

3 teaspoons grated bouillon cube

1 heaping tablespoon flour

^{1}/2 teaspoon garam masala

1 teaspoon butter

^{1}/2 teaspoon salt

1 teaspoon turmeric powder

1 tablespoon marmalade

1. Place the potato, unpeeled, in the Cook-Zen. Cover and heat on medium-high for 5 minutes with the steam holes set to "close." After cooking, peel the potato, cut into bite-size pieces, and set aside.

2. Place the olive oil and garlic in the Cook-Zen. Heat on medium-high, uncovered, for 30 seconds.

3. Add the onion, celery, ginger, carrot, eggplant, mushrooms, broccoli, and meat to the Cook-Zen. Cover and heat on medium-high for 10 minutes with the steam holes set to "close."

4. Add the water, curry powder, cayenne pepper, grated bouillon, flour, garam masala, butter, salt, turmeric, and marmalade to the Cook-Zen and mix well. Cover and heat on medium-high for 10 minutes with the steam holes set to "close." Add the potato and mix gently before serving.

Asian-Style Spareribs

4 servings
Cook Time: 14 minutes

4 teaspoons olive oil

2 cloves garlic, sliced

8 pork ribs (about 1^1/2 pounds)

4 tablespoons ketchup

2 tablespoons soy sauce

2 tablespoons sugar

Place the olive oil and garlic in the Cook-Zen. Heat on medium-high, uncovered, for 1 minute. Add the remaining ingredients and mix well. Cover and heat on medium-high for 13 minutes with the steam holes set to "close."

Stuffed Calamari

2 servings
Cook Time: 3¹/3 minutes

2 plum tomatoes
2 (2-ounce) squid, cleaned
4 fresh basil leaves
2 anchovy fillets
Pinch of salt and black pepper
Parmesan cheese, grated, for garnish

1. Cut the tomatoes into ¹/2-inch slices. Stuff each squid with the slices from 1 tomato, 2 basil leaves, and 1 anchovy fillet. Close the ends of the squid with a tooth pick.

2. Place both stuffed squid inside the Cook-Zen, and lightly sprinkle with salt and pepper. Cover and heat on medium-high for 3 to 3¹/3 minutes with the steam holes set to "close." Sprinkle the squid with Parmesan cheese before serving.

Simmered Beef

2 servings
Cook Time: 8 minutes

Gyudon, a popular dish in Japan, consists of beef simmered in soy sauce and mirin served over a bowl of rice. This version gives you all the traditional flavors in a fraction of the traditional cooking time.

1 large onion, halved and sliced
$^1/_2$ pound beef round, thinly sliced
$2^1/_2$ to 3 tablespoons soy sauce
2 tablespoons mirin
$1^1/_2$ tablespoons sugar
1 tablespoon water

Place all ingredients in the Cook-Zen. Lightly mix. Cover and heat on medium-high for 7 to 8 minutes with the steam holes set to "close." Serve the beef with sauce over a bowl of rice (see recipe, page 118).

Beef Round Steak with Garlic

1 serving
Cook Time: 2 minutes

1 teaspoon olive oil

1/3 pound boneless beef round steak

1 clove garlic, sliced

Pinch of salt and black pepper

Place olive oil, beef, garlic, salt, and pepper in the Cook-Zen. Cover and heat on medium-high for 1 1/2 minutes for rare, 2 minutes for medium, with the steam holes set to "close." Arrange the beef on a plate and top with tangy steak sauce (see page 30).

Salmon Teriyaki

1 serving
Cook Time: 3 minutes

1 (¹/2-pound) salmon fillet, with skin

3 tablespoons soy sauce

1 tablespoon sugar

1 to 2 tablespoons mirin

Place the salmon in the Cook-Zen, and add the soy sauce, sugar, and mirin. Heat on medium-high for 2¹/2 to 3 minutes with the steam holes set to "close." Serve over rice or with a vegetable such as broccoli or bok choy.

Spicy Coconut Chicken

2 servings
Cook Time: 9 minutes

$^1/_3$ pound boneless chicken breast, cubed

Pinch of salt

$^1/_2$ large onion, sliced

1 tablespoon minced garlic

1 tablespoon minced ginger

1 tablespoon olive oil

$^2/_3$ Cook-Zen cup coconut milk

1 teaspoon garam masala

$^1/_2$ to 1 teaspoon chili powder, or to taste

Pinch of cayenne pepper

$^1/_2$ teaspoon turmeric powder

$^1/_2$ tablespoon sugar

1. Sprinkle the chicken with salt and set aside. Place the onion, garlic, ginger, and olive oil in the Cook-Zen. Cover and heat on medium-high for 3 minutes with the steam holes set to "close."

2. Add the chicken and remaining ingredients to the Cook-Zen and mix well. Cover and heat on medium-high for 6 minutes with the steam holes set to "close."

Side Dishes

White Rice

Steamed Artichoke

Glazed Carrot

Greek-Style Spinach Rice

Parmesan Risotto

Baked Leeks with Butter-Soy Sauce

Herbed Potatoes

Couscous with Tomato, Onion, and Cucumber

Baked Tomato with Parmesan and Parsley

White and Green Asparagus Salad

Creamy Kabocha Pumpkin

Garlic Cauliflower with Bacon

Classic Mashed Potatoes

Sweet and Sour Cabbage

Mixed Vegetable Sauté with Basil-Oregano
   Tomato Sauce

Rosemary Mushrooms and Zucchini

Potatoes in Spicy Green Chile Sauce

Barbecue Baked Beans

Baby Spinach and Tomato Sauté

Steamed Beet

Steamed Onion

White Rice

*Makes 5 Cook-Zen cups
of rice, about 3 servings
Cook Time: 16 minutes*

2 Cook-Zen cups Japanese white rice
2^1/2 Cook-Zen cups water

1. Place the rice in the Cook-Zen, add fresh cold water to cover, and swish the rice around to wash. Drain and repeat several times until the water runs clear.

2. Drain the rice well. Add 2^1/2 Cook-Zen cups water. Let the rice soak for 1 hour. Do not drain. Cover and heat on medium-high for 15 to 16 minutes with the steam holes set to "open." Let stand for 5 minutes.

Note: You can substitute any type of rice in this recipe, as long as it's not instant rice or mochi sweet rice. Brown, jasmine, and basmati all work well.

Steamed Artichoke

1 serving
Cook Time: 9 minutes

1 artichoke (about $^1/_2$ pound)

Wash the artichoke and place in the Cook-Zen. Cover and heat on medium-high for 8 to 9 minutes with the steam holes set to "close." Serve with melted butter or mayonaisse for dipping, if desired.

Glazed Carrot

2 servings
Cook Time: $3^1/_2$ minutes

1 large carrot, peeled and cut into $^1/_2$-inch slices
2 tablespoons water
$^1/_2$ tablespoon sugar
Pinch of salt

Place all the ingredients in the Cook-Zen. Cover and heat on medium-high for 3 to $3^1/_2$ minutes with the steam holes set to "close."

Greek-Style Spinach Rice

4 servings
Cook Time: 18 minutes

2 Cook-Zen cups rice
2¹/2 Cook-Zen cups water
5 to 6 ounces baby spinach, rinsed
2 tablespoons butter
2 teaspoons grated bouillon cube, any flavor
Pinch of sugar

1. Place the rice in the Cook-Zen, add fresh cold water to cover, and swish the rice around to wash. Drain and repeat several times until the water runs clear. Drain the rice well. Add 2¹/2 Cook-Zen cups water and let soak for 1 hour. Do not drain.

2. Add the remaining ingredients to the Cook-Zen with the rice. Cover and heat on medium-high for 17 to 18 minutes with the steam holes set to "open." Stir well before serving.

Parmesan Risotto

2 to 4 servings
Cook Time: 12 minutes

1 teaspoon olive oil

1 tablespoon butter

$^1/2$ medium onion, finely chopped

2 Cook-Zen cups cooked rice (see recipe, page 118)

2 Cook-Zen cups water

1 teaspoon grated bouillon cube, any flavor

Pinch of salt

Pinch of sugar

2 tablespoons Parmesan cheese, grated

1. Place the olive oil, butter, and onion in the Cook-Zen. Cover and heat on medium-high for 2 minutes with the steam holes set to "close."

2. Add the rice, water, grated bouillon, salt, and sugar. Cover and heat on medium-high for 10 minutes with the steam holes set to "open." Add the Parmesan and mix well.

Variations:

Mushroom Risotto: Slice 6 mushrooms, any kind. Prepare the risotto as directed above, adding the mushrooms to the Cook-Zen at the same time as the rice, water, grated bouillon, salt, and sugar. Finish as directed.

Asparagus Risotto: Cut five asparagus stalks into 1-inch slices. Prepare the risotto as directed above. Add the asparagus to the Cook-Zen at the same time as the rice, water, grated bouillon, salt, and sugar. Finish as directed.

Baked Leeks with Butter-Soy Sauce

2 servings
Cook Time: 6 minutes

If you prefer more of the natural flavor of leeks, replace the butter and soy sauce with salt and pepper.

2 leeks
1 tablespoon butter, room temperature
1 tablespoon soy sauce

1. Wash the leeks until all the grit is removed. Cut away the upper dark green parts of the leeks, removing the hard part. Cut leeks into 2-inch lengths and then julienne.

2. Place the leeks in the Cook-Zen, cover, and heat on medium-high for 5 to 6 minutes with the steam holes set to "close." After heating, add the butter and soy sauce. Mix well.

Herbed
Potatoes

4 servings
Cook Time: 8 minutes

2 medium potatoes, any kind
Pinch of black pepper
1 sprig rosemary, chopped
Pinch of dried oregano
Pinch of dried thyme
Pinch of dried sage
Pinch of dried marjoram
Pinch of salt

1. Place the potatoes, unpeeled, in the Cook-Zen. Cover and heat on medium-high for 7 to 8 minutes with the steam holes set to "close." After heating, peel the potatoes and cut into bite-size pieces.

2. On a baking sheet, mix the black pepper, rosemary, oregano, thyme, sage, and marjoram. Place the potatoes on the baking sheet while still hot and coat with the mixed herbs. Sprinkle lightly with salt before serving.

Couscous with Tomato, Onion, and Cucumber

2 servings
Cook Time: 6^{1}/2 minutes

^{1}/3 cup couscous
1 tablespoon butter
Pinch of salt and black pepper
^{1}/2 cup water
^{1}/2 medium onion
1 plum tomato
1 medium cucumber
Dash of lemon juice
Pinch of sugar

1. Place the couscous, butter, salt, pepper, and water in the Cook-Zen. Cover and heat on medium-high for 1 to 1^{1}/2 minutes with the steam holes set to "close." Let cool, about 10 minutes.

2. Finely chop the onion and soak it in a bowl of water for 5 minutes; drain. Chop the tomato and cucumber into ^{1}/4-inch cubes.

3. In a large mixing bowl, combine all ingredients. Toss well.

Baked Tomato with Parmesan and Parsley

1 serving
Cook Time: 2 minutes

1 plum tomato, halved
Parmesan cheese, grated
Italian parsley or chives, chopped

Place the tomato halves in the Cook-Zen. Cover and heat on medium-high for 1$\frac{1}{2}$ to 2 minutes with the steam holes set to "close." Sprinkle with cheese and parsley before serving.

White and Green Asparagus Salad

2 *servings*
Cook Time: 3 *minutes*

4 stalks green asparagus
4 stalks white asparagus
1 tablespoon finely chopped onion
$^1/_2$ cup mayonnaise
1 tablespoon white vinegar
1 tablespoon mirin

1. Remove the hard leaves and root area from the asparagus. Cut the asparagus stalks in half, and place them in the Cook-Zen. Cover and heat on medium-high for 2 to 3 minutes, depending on the size of your asparagus, until tender, with the steam holes set to "close." Rinse under cool water after heating.

2. In a small mixing bowl, combine the remaining ingredients. Pour the dressing over the asparagus to serve.

Creamy Kabocha Pumpkin

4 servings
Cook Time: 6 minutes

1 pound kabocha pumpkin
2 to 3 tablespoons mayonnaise
2 to 3 tablespoons heavy cream
Pinch of sugar

1. Seed the pumpkin, cut into 1-inch cubes and place in the Cook-Zen. Cover and heat on medium-high for 5 to 6 minutes with the steam holes set to "close."

2. Transfer the pumpkin to a medium mixing bowl and let cool. Peel the skin from the pumpkin and discard. Add the mayonnaise, cream, and sugar and gently mix.

Garlic Cauliflower with Bacon

2 servings
Cook Time: 9 minutes

1 small head cauliflower (about $^3/4$ pound)

2 tablespoons minced garlic

1 tablespoon olive oil

1 slice bacon, finely chopped

$^1/2$ teaspoon grated bouillon cube, any flavor

1. Chop the cauliflower into florets.

2. Place the garlic and olive oil in the Cook-Zen. Cover and heat on medium-high for 1 minute with the steam holes set to "close."

3. Add the cauliflower, bacon, and grated bouillon to the garlic and olive oil in the Cook-Zen. Stir, then cover and heat on medium-high for 8 minutes with the steam holes set to "close."

Classic Mashed Potatoes

4 servings
Cook Time: 8 to 9 minutes

2 medium potatoes
1 teaspoon butter
Pinch of salt

1. Place the potatoes, unpeeled, in the Cook-Zen. Cover and heat on medium-high for 8 to 9 minutes with the steam holes set to "close."

2. After heating, peel the skin, and place the potato back inside the Cook-Zen. Using a spatula or a wooden spoon, flatten the potato. Add the butter and salt, and mash until smooth.

Sweet and Sour Cabbage

4 servings
Cook Time: 5 minutes

$1/2$ head cabbage, thinly julienned
4 tablespoons white wine vinegar
2 tablespoons sugar
1 tablespoon olive oil
Pinch of salt

1. Place the cabbage in the Cook-Zen, cover, and heat on medium-high for 4 to 5 minutes with the steam holes set to "close."

2. Rinse the cabbage under the cool water, drain, and let cool.

3. In a medium bowl, toss the cabbage with the vinegar, sugar, olive oil, and salt until the cabbage is well coated.

Mixed Vegetable Sauté with Basil-Oregano Tomato Sauce

2 servings
Cook Time: 5 minutes

1 small zucchini
2 Japanese eggplants or 1 small American eggplant
6 pearl onions
2 mushrooms, any kind
2 tablespoons olive oil
2 cloves garlic, minced
2 tablespoons tomato puree
2 tablespoons ketchup
Pinch of dried oregano
10 fresh basil leaves or pinch of dried basil
1 teaspoon grated bouillon cube, any flavor
1 teaspoon sugar
Pinch of salt and black pepper

1. Cut the zucchini and eggplants into $1/2$-inch thick pieces. Peel and halve the onions. Cut the mushrooms into 1-inch slices.

2. Place the olive oil and garlic in the Cook-Zen. Heat on medium-high, uncovered, for 40 seconds.

3. Add all the ingredients to the olive oil and garlic. Mix well. Cover and heat on medium-high for 4 minutes with the steam holes set to "close."

Rosemary Mushrooms and Zucchini

2 servings
Cook Time: 6 minutes

6 white or cremini mushrooms
2 king oyster mushrooms
3 shiitake mushrooms
1 small zucchini
1 tablespoon olive oil
1 tablespoon butter
1 clove garlic, thinly sliced
Pinch of salt and black pepper
1 sprig rosemary
Dash of soy sauce

1. Slice the mushrooms and zucchini in $1/2$-inch slices.

2. Place the olive oil, butter, and sliced garlic inside the Cook-Zen and heat on medium-high, uncovered, for 40 seconds.

3. Add the mushrooms, zucchini, salt, pepper, and rosemary to the Cook-Zen. Cover and heat on medium-high for 4 to 5 minutes with the steam holes set to "close." Mix in a dash of soy sauce before serving.

Potatoes in Spicy Green Chile Sauce

2 servings
Cook Time: 9 minutes

2 tablespoons olive oil

1 clove garlic, minced

2 large Japanese green chile peppers or jalapeño peppers, seeds removed and finely chopped (see Note)

1 plum tomato, finely chopped

1/4 medium onion, finely chopped

Pinch of sugar

Pinch of salt and black pepper

1 large potato, any kind

1. Place the olive oil, garlic, peppers, tomato, and onion in the Cook-Zen; mix well. Cover and heat on medium-high for 3 minutes with the steam holes set to "close." Add a pinch of sugar, salt, and pepper, and mix well. Transfer the sauce to a medium mixing bowl.

2. Place the potato, unpeeled, in the Cook-Zen. Cover and heat on medium-high for 5 to 6 minutes with the steam holes set to "close." After heating, peel the skin and cut the potatoes into 1-inch cubes. While the potatoes are still hot, add to the sauce. Mix gently.

Note: Be careful when working with chiles; the natural oils can burn. Don't touch your eyes, and wash your hands immediately after handling.

Barbecue Baked Beans

4 servings
Cook Time: 12^1/2
minutes

2 cloves garlic, minced

1 tablespoon olive oil

1 medium onion, finely chopped

3 tablespoons ketchup

2 tablespoons soy sauce

1 tablespoon white wine vinegar

2 tablespoons honey

1 small apple, core removed and grated

^{1}/2 teaspoon black pepper

2 teaspoons yellow mustard

^{1}/2 teaspoon dried tarragon

1 (15-ounce) can cannellini or navy beans, rinsed and drained

1. Place the garlic and olive oil inside the Cook-Zen and heat on medium-high for 30 seconds uncovered. Add the remaining ingredients except the beans to the Cook-Zen, cover, and heat on medium-high for 10 minutes with the steam holes set to "close."

2. Add the beans to the Cook-Zen, mix well while the sauce is still hot. Cover and heat on medium-high for 2 minutes with the steam holes set to "close." Mix well before serving.

Baby Spinach and Tomato Sauté

2 servings
Cook Time: 4 minutes

2 plum tomatoes, diced
10 ounces baby spinach, rinsed
2 anchovy fillets
1 tablespoon olive oil
2 tablespoons ketchup
$^1/2$ tablespoon sugar

Place all ingredients in the Cook-Zen. Mix well. Cover and heat on medium-high for 3 to 4 minutes with the steam holes set to "close."

Steamed Beet

2 *servings*
Cook Time: 8 *minutes*

1 beet (about $^3/4$ pound)

Place the beet, unpeeled, in the Cook-Zen. Cover and heat on medium-high for 8 minutes with the steam holes set to "close." Peel and cut into 1-inch cubes before serving.

Steamed Onion

2 *servings*
Cook Time: 3 *minutes*

1 large onion
Soy sauce, optional
Salt, optional
Ketchup, optional

Place the onion, unpeeled, in the Cook-Zen. Cover and heat on medium-high for 3 minutes with the steam holes set to "close." Remove the peel and cut the onion into slices. Dip in soy sauce, salt, or ketchup.

Desserts

Lemon Mousse

Banana Pudding

Chocolate Truffles

Sweet Simmered Figs

Panna Cotta with Fresh Berries

Baked Apple with Honey

Lemon Mousse

2 servings
Cook Time: 2 minutes
plus 3 hours for cooling

3 tablespoons water
1 teaspoon gelatin powder
1/2 stick butter (4 tablespoons)
1 egg, yolk separated
1/4 Cook-Zen cup sugar plus 2 tablespoons
Juice of *1/2 lemon*
1/2 Cook-Zen cup heavy cream

1. In a small, microwave-safe bowl, mix the water and gelatin and heat on medium-high, uncovered, for 30 seconds. Set aside.

2. Place the butter in the Cook-Zen, cover, and heat on medium-high for 30 seconds with the steam holes set to "close."

3. In a large mixing bowl, whisk the egg yolk until smooth. Add 1/4 Cook-Zen cup sugar and lemon juice; whisk well. Slowly stir the yolk mixture into the Cook-Zen with the melted butter, cover, and heat on medium high for 1 minute with the steam holes set to "close."

4. In a separate large bowl, beat the heavy cream with a hand mixer while adding 1 tablespoon of sugar, until the cream is light and fluffy.

5. In a small bowl, beat the egg white and 1 tablespoon sugar until peaks form. Add the gelatin, heavy cream mixture, and egg white to the Cook-Zen, and swiftly cut together. Do not stir. Pour the mixture into a small cake mold and let it set in the refrigerator, about 3 hours. Serve in the mold, or invert onto a serving dish.

Banana Pudding

4 servings
Cook Time: 1¹/2 minutes
plus 3 hours for cooling

2 bananas, chopped
4 ounces mascarpone cheese
¹/2 Cook-Zen cup water
1 teaspoon gelatin powder
5 tablespoons sugar
1 Cook-Zen cup heavy cream

1. Place the bananas in a blender and blend until smooth. Add the mascarpone, and blend until incorporated.

2. In the Cook-Zen, mix the water and gelatin. Cover and heat on medium-high for 1¹/2 minutes with the steam holes set to "close." Add the sugar, cream, and banana mixture, and mix well. Refrigerate for 3 hours before serving.

Chocolate Truffles

16 to 18 truffles
Cook Time: 1 minute
plus 4 hours for cooling

¹/4 pound semi-sweet chocolate, grated
¹/4 Cook-Zen cup heavy cream
¹/2 stick (4 tablespoons) salted butter
1 tablespoon brandy
Cocoa powder, for coating the truffles

1. Place the chocolate, heavy cream, and butter in the Cook-Zen. Cover and heat on medium-high for 50 seconds with the steam holes set to "open." The chocolate should not be fully melted. Whisk the ingredients together until smooth. Add the brandy, and continue whisking until the texture thickens. Place chocolate in the refrigerator to cool, about 1 hour.

2. Remove the chocolate from the refrigerator once it begins to harden. Cover a flat surface with a thin layer of cocoa powder. Roll the chocolate into 1-inch balls with your hands then roll the chocolate balls through the cocoa powder, making sure they're fully coated.

3. Store the truffles in an airtight container. Pack the container with cocoa powder and refrigerate for 3 hours before serving.

Sweet Simmered Figs

2 servings
Cook Time: 5 minutes

8 figs
1 cup water
2 teaspoons lemon juice
5 tablespoons sugar
Splash of milk, optional

1. Place the figs, unpeeled, in the Cook-Zen. Add the water, lemon juice, and sugar, and mix gently. Cover and heat on medium-high for 4 to 5 minutes with the steam holes set to "close."

2. Place the figs in bowls to serve, distributing the liquid from the Cook-Zen evenly into the bowls. Serve warm or chilled with a splash of cold milk, if desired.

Panna Cotta with Fresh Berries

2 servings

Cook Time: 2^{1}/$_{2}$ minutes

plus 2 hours for cooling

^{1}/$_{2}$ Cook-Zen cup heavy cream

^{1}/$_{2}$ Cook-Zen cup milk

2 tablespoons powdered sugar

^{1}/$_{2}$ teaspoon gelatin powder

3 tablespoons water

Fresh berries, optional

1. In the Cook-Zen, whisk together the heavy cream, milk, and powdered sugar. Cover and heat on medium-high for 1^{1}/$_{2}$ to 2 minutes with the steam holes set to "close."

2. In a small, microwave-safe bowl, mix the gelatin powder and water. Heat on medium-high for 20 to 30 seconds. Add the gelatin mixture to the contents of the Cook-Zen and stir well.

3. Divide the mixture into two small bowls or cooking molds and let cool in the refrigerator for 2 hours. Serve in the molds or invert onto serving dishes. Garnish with fresh berries if desired.

Baked Apple
with Honey

2 servings
Cook Time: 5 minutes

1 red apple, core removed and cut into 6 slices
3 to 4 tablespoons honey

Place the slices inside the Cook-Zen, cover, and heat on medium-high for 4 to 5 minutes with the steam holes set to "close." Drizzle the apple slices with honey. Serve with vanilla ice cream, if desired.

Index

C

cabbage:
  baked or boiled sausages with, 97
  Napa, bacon soup, smoky, 58
  sweet and sour, 134
calamari, stuffed, 108
caramelized onion soup with mozzarella, 50
carrot, glazed, 119
cauliflower:
  garlic, with bacon, 133
  soup, sweet, 53
cayenne pepper, in yellow curry, 104–5
celery, in Adriatic chicken-meatball stew, 61
cheese:
  mascarpone, in banana pudding, 147
  mozzarella, caramelized onion soup with, 50
  see also Parmesan
chicken:
  basil, and anchovy sauté, 93
  curry with spinach and apple, 88
  lime garlic, 83
  -meatball stew, Adriatic, 61
  red wine stew with olives, cranberries and, 72
  spicy coconut, 115
  Thai green curry, 98
  with tomato-basil sauce, 96
chickpeas, in hummus with mushrooms, peppers, and almonds, 36
chile pepper:
  red, in Adriatic chicken-meatball stew, 61
  in spicy chilled tomato soup, 57
chile sauce, spicy green, potatoes in, 138
chili con carne, 71
chili paste, in spicy shrimp with peas, 101
chili powder, 18
  in spicy coconut chicken, 115
chives, Asian, in Korean beef bulgogi, 78
chocolate truffles, 148
chowder:
  clam, 55
  corn, 73
chutney, lemon-apple, 22
clam:
  chowder, 55
  tomato sauce, 33
classic mashed potatoes, 134
coconut chicken, spicy, 115
coconut milk, in spicy chilled tomato soup, 57
Cook-Zen Cookbook, The (Chiba), 11

Cook-Zen pot, 11, 16
  how to use, 17
  reasons to use, 15
corn chowder, 73
couscous with tomato, onion, and cucumber, 126
cranberries, red wine stew with chicken, olives and, 72
cream cheese, in spinach artichoke dip, 41
creamy:
  dill shrimp, 80
  kabocha pumpkin, 131
  kabocha pumpkin soup, 48
  tomato artichoke sauce, 23
  tomato soup with potatoes, 63
cucumber, couscous with tomato, onion and, 126
curry:
  chicken, Thai green, 98
  chicken, with spinach and apple, 88
  yellow, 104–5

D

daikon, in Asian vegetable and bacon soup, 52
desserts, 146–53
  baked apple with honey, 153
  banana pudding, 147
  chocolate truffles, 148
  lemon mousse, 146
  panna cotta with fresh berries, 152
  sweet simmered figs, 151
dill, shrimp, creamy, 80
dip, spinach artichoke, 41

E

eggplant:
  in mixed vegetable sauté with basil-oregano tomato sauce, 135
  spread, Turkish, 37
  in Thai green curry chicken, 98
  in yellow curry, 104–5

F

fennel garlic soup, 56
figs, sweet simmered, 151
fish:
  in paella, 103
  salmon teriyaki, 112
  salmon with lemon-soy sauce, 89
  sea bass pot-au-feu, 87
  see also seafood; shellfish